THE SIMPLE
PROPHECY
HANDBOOK

IDENTIFYING THE PROPHETIC
GIFTING IN YOU

REV. DR. SANDRA Y. WASHINGTON

ISBN: 979-8-89465-000-5 (sc)
ISBN: 979-8-89465-001-2 (e)

Printed in the United States of America.

Integrity Publishing
39343 Harbor Hills Blvd Lady Lake,
FL 32159

www.integrity-publishing.com

CONTENTS

THE ACKNOWLEDGEMENT

Many thanks to my mentors who attributed to my growth in the prophetic ministry, such as, Jesus Christ, the true Prophet, who gave and continues to give me revelatory messages, through visions, dreams, perception and wisdom according to His will. Many thanks to additional mentors who helped develop the gift of the prophetic ministry, such as, prophet and teacher, Bill Hamon, CEO of Christian International School of Theology in Santa Rosa Beach, FL., Prophetess Teresa Gripper, CEO of the prophetic school called "Naioth Prophetical Arts Institute" in Brooklyn, N.Y., B Prophet James Goll, pastor of the God Encounter Ministries and who wrote the book, "The Prophet", and lastly, Pastor and teacher of the prophetic seer anointing, Barbara Rispoli, pastor of Healing Waters Church in Selden, N.Y.

If I can recall, there were other mentors who conducted prophetic schools in my early years of prophetic growth, such as, Rev. Christopher Cox in Elmont, N.Y. whose prophetic presbytery anointed me in the area of prophecy through music, and Apostle and Prophetess Pauline Walley-Daniels in Bronx, N.Y. who taught about the process of being a Prophet. She is also the teacher of spiritual warfare deliverance ministry.

THE INTRODUCTION

Jesus Christ has inspired me to write this handbook on the various methods of prophecy to use as a resource for those believers in Christ, whom God has called into the prophetic ministry, and who wish to learn and develop in the prophetic ministry. This handbook is also for those believers who just want to know about the prophetic ministry and how it operates in prophetic people.

This handbook will cover the definition of prophecy and the various methods of prophecy such as, the Spirit of prophecy, the gift of prophecy, the prophetic preaching, the prophetic presbytery, the seer prophet and the office of a prophet. The reader of this handbook will learn that in the area of the office of a prophet there is a *Nabi prophet*, of which there are two types of *Nabi prophets*, and a prophetic watchman called a *Shamar*. These various methods of prophecy will be defined in more detail as the reader continues to read this handbook. There are three types of prophets, the Seer Prophet, the Office of a Prophet and the Prophet Shamar or the Watchman who Intercedes.

This handbook will discuss the tasks of a prophet and how the other prophetic methods operate within the believers in Christ. Before anyone can operate in any level or method of the prophetic, one must be saved - who has accepted Jesus as their personal Savior, be baptized in the Holy Spirit, with the evidence of speaking a supernatural language, or filled with the Spirit of God to be more effective prophetically. You can still prophesy if you are just saved in Christ, because you still received the Holy Spirit within you.

In order to release a prophetic word as an ordinary believer, every believer must learn how to hear God and know that he speaks in various ways. This handbook will help you know how to identify God's voice and how to use the measure of faith you received at salvation.

Learning how to hear God takes practice, so you will make some mistakes when prophesying. If that happens, repent and learn through your mistakes. You will find you will get better at prophesying as you grow prophetically. God knows you are growing prophetically and sees the sincerity of your heart to want to be a spokesman for him. He will not condemn you if you make a mistake every once in a while when prophesying. Just continue to practice prophesying exactly what you are feeling God is impressing in your spirit to say, or what you are hearing by a still small voice of the Holy Spirit, who is God. Say exactly what he says. Don't ever add to what He says to you or to anyone else. Journal what God says. This handbook will teach you the various ways God speaks. Whatever He says to you, must line up with the Word of God, The Bible.

It is hoped that when you finish reading this prophetic handbook, you will know how to identify God's voice within you and without you through other believers and circumstances. How to release a personal or corporate prophetic messages through activation exercises, as well as identifying what method of prophecy God operates within you, also through activation exercises.

The purpose of this handbook is to help develop the prophetic giftings within believers who read this handbook. It is believed that it is God's will to raise up a company of prophets in these last days of the end times, when the world system is so chaotic and divided. Believers in Christ need to know how to hear God for wisdom, counsel, and direction, when dealing with unbelievers who don't know the God of Jesus Christ, whom the Christians serve. It is up to the remnant believers in Christ to be a positive influence to peoples' lives and reflect the light of Christ in love towards people who have no spiritual discernment. However, believers in Christ can give them hope by giving them a prophetic word of encouragement from Jesus Christ, or from God within you as he inspires you to speak or pray for the people.

It is hoped that this *Simple Prophetic Ministrying Handbook* will be a blessing to whoever reads this book. May God bless you all.

CHAPTER 1

WHAT IS PROPHECY?

Prophecy is the inspired word of God spoken through any believer in Christ to another person, group of people or to a church congregation. It is an encouraging message from God, usually pertaining to the life of the one giving the message or to encourage another person or group. Prophecy is also the inspired word of God through which the Holy Spirit reveals the heart and will of God to mankind through the spirit of any believer in Christ or any fivefold minister in the body of Christ according to the written word of God, 1Corinthians 2: 9,10 (NLT), "No eye has not seen, no ear has heard, and no mind have imagined what God has prepared for those who love Him." "But we know these things because God has revealed them to us by His Spirit and His Spirit searches out everything and shows even God's deep secrets."

    Prophecy has two dimensions: 1. Forthtelling Prophecy – A Christian is inspired by the Holy Spirit to give a recipient or group of people a message from God to edify, exhort or comfort at that present moment. **2. Foretelling Prophecy**- A Christian is inspired by the Holy Spirit to give to a recipient a prophecy that is in conjunction with the gift of Word of Wisdom to give the prophecy a futuristic revelation knowledge concerning God's will and plan for the recipient's life or for a leader of a nation, family member or unbeliever, John 16:13b, (NLT), "He, the Holy Spirit will show you the future."

WHAT DOES PROPHECY DO?

1. Prophecy can give instruction (2 Timothy 3:16, John 14:26)
2. Prophecy inspires faith (Hebrews 11:1)
3. Prophecy increases faith (Romans 10:17, Hebrews 11: 1)
4. Prophecy, along with the word of wisdom, reveals the future (John 16: 13)
5. Prophecy has creative power that brings life (Ezekiel 37: 1-14)
6. Prophecy makes the simple wise, because you will know what to do (John 14: 26 & John 16: 13)
7. Prophecy can become a living sword against the enemy, Satan (Matt. 2: 7-16, Ephesians 6: 13 -18)

WHAT IS THE MAIN TASK OF PROPHECY?

In 1 Corinthians 14:3 says, "But he who prophesies speaks edification and exhortation and comfort to me." Even though believers operate in this prophetic gift, it is important to have good character and walk in love with humility. It says in 1 Corinthians 13:1-4(EBV), "If I speak in the tongues of men and of angels, but have not love, I am a noisy gong and a clanging cymbal; and if I have prophetic powers, and understand all mysteries and all knowledge and if I have all faith so as to remove mountains and have not love, I am nothing. If I give away all I have, If I deliver my body to be burned, but have not love, I gain nothing."

"Love is patient and kind; love is not jealous or boastful, it is not arrogant or rude. Love does not insist on its own way; it is not irritable or resentful; it does not rejoice in the wrong, but rejoices in the right. Love bears all things, believes all things, hopes all things and endures all things."

To be an effective deliverer of God's prophetic message to others, use your discernment to pray about the prophetic message, or be led of the Lord to deliver the message, but make sure you deliver in love and not with condemnation. Ask God what to do with the message He reveals to you. Your message is to edify or build up the self-esteem and hope of the person

2

You should exhort or encourage the person whose on the right path of righteousness. if your prophetic message is a warning to the person, say it in love and be assertive. Comfort the person who may be in despair over the loss of a loved one, giving him hope to continue living on to be productive.

Prophecy can be spoken in a heavenly language called *tongues,* during your devotional time alone with God or with Jesus Christ. Your spiritual language is a supernatural gift given to every believer who is baptized in the Holy Spirit after receiving salvation. It is God's way of establishing a closer relationship with you and you with Him. He will anoint you or empower you by His Holy Spirit to operate in the spiritual gifts, of which one of them is prophesying. and do the works that Jesus did and even greater works. Jesus says in John 14: 12-14, "Truly, truly, I say to you, he (or she) who believes in Me will also do the works that I do and greater works than these will he do because I go to the Father. Whatever you ask in my name, I will do it that the Father may be glorified in the Son. If you ask anything in My Name, I will do it."

So, if you are not baptized in the Holy Spirit, just tell God that you desire more of Him and ask Him to fill you with His Holy Spirit with the evidence of speaking in tongues. Once He knows you are sincere from the heart, by faith, expecting His full presence to fill you, He will give you exactly what you asked for. Take a deep breath with your mouth open and when you sense a moving of the Holy Spirit in your belly, just give the Holy Spirit your voice and tongue making babbling sounds. Don't worry what comes out of your mouth; you won't understand it anyway. Just speak out the language in faith and know it is the Holy Spirit, praying in tongues through you, unto God. Know that you are baptized in the Holy Spirit by faith.

Paul says in 1 Corinthians 14:1-5 (EBV), "Make love your aim and earnestly desire the spiritual gifts, especially that you may prophesy. For one who speaks in a tongue speaks not to men but to God; for no one understands him but he utters mysteries in the Spirit (this is the spirit-filled believer's devotional tongue or prayer tongue). On the other hand, he who prophesies speaks to men for their upbuilding (edification), encouragement (exhortation) and consolation (comfort). He who speaks in a tongue edifies himself, but he who prophesies edifies the church. Now I want you all to prophesy. He who prophesies is greater than he who speaks in tongues, unless someone (another spirit-filled believer) interprets so that the church may be edified." In this case, Paul is saying if a spirit-filled believer speaks in tongues to a congregation, they will not be able to understand the prophecy in tongues, unless a sensitive spirit-filled believer interprets what was said in tongues. Then the congregation will be edified by the interpretation. The person who gave the message in tongues was operating by the utterance gift of the Holy Spirit, called the *gift of diverse tongues,* and the person who gave the interpretation was operating by the utterance gift called the *gift of interpretation.* Sometimes, the interpretation can operate through the person who prophesied in tongues. Either way, prophecy spoken in tongues to a group, or to a congregation must have the gift of interpretation following it, in order for the message in tongues to be understood.

CHAPTER 2

VARIOUS WAYS GOD SPEAKS TO YOU

Every believer can hear the voice of God whether he or she knows it or not. Jesus said in His word in John 10:27, "My sheep (believers in Christ) hear my voice. And I know them and they follow Me." However, there are times when some believers are not sure they can hear the Lord when He speaks. When a believer is unsure that he or she can hear God, it is important to spend time in the presence of God by establishing a devotional time with Him. Read scriptures that tell of His character and how He spoke to people mainly through prophets in stories indicated in the Old and New Testaments. During your devotional time, ask the Holy Spirit to help you pray in the Spirit (in tongues) or in your native language. This practice will edify you to being more sensitive to the presence of God and to the promptings or urges of the Holy Spirit who is the voice of God. Once you practice spending time in the presence of God, you will be able to identify when He speaks to you. You will be able to prophesy more effectively of what He says to you and to another person through you.

God can speak to you in various ways. They are as follows:

- **INWARD KNOWING:** You can identify how God speaks to you inwardly or within you by the Holy Spirit. Remember, the Holy Spirit is the voice of God. He will speak within your human spirit, which is the heart of man, or in this case to the believer. The heart of the believer in Christ is a redeemed spirit that was purged or cleansed from the sin nature by the shed blood of Jesus, when the believer accepted the redemptive work of Christ on the cross. Therefore, the Holy Spirit, also called the Spirit of truth, lives and abides within you (the believer) forever to guide you into all truth, teach you all things, direct you and show you things to come. John 14:26 and John 16:13. You automatically have an inward knowing, an inward witness, or an intuition that something will happen or what was hoped for or expected, will soon come to pass.

- **A STILL SMALL VOICE:** The Holy Spirit or God Himself can quicken a word or phrase in your human spirit, spoken in your native language, called *"the still small voice"*. You may hear a soft whisper or low voice saying to you "blessings are coming," or "I am coming." You may even hear God call your name like He called Samuel's name when Samuel was a young lad in 1 Samuel 3:1-9. You may hear a person's name in your spirit; either you are to pray for that person, call that person or you even may hear from that person.

- **REVELATORY DREAMS AND VISIONS:** Do not take your dreams and visions for granted. Dreams come when you are sleeping and visions come when you are awake; they are called open visions. A trance is when you are half awake or in a twilight state unaware of your surroundings. Sometimes you may experience an out of body state. In the trance, God may or may not speak as He reveals a vision to reveal a mission or a teaching.

When you become too busy and don't have time to commune with God, God will find the time to communicate with you. One of the ways is through dreams and visions. God says in Job 33:15-18, "In a dream, in a vision of the night, when deep sleep falls upon men, while they slumber on their beds, then He opens the ears of men and terrifies them with warnings that He may turn man aside from his (evil) deed and cut off pride from man; He keeps back his soul from the Pit (of Hell) and his life from perishing by the sword." Therefore, God speaks through dreams and visions to bring instruction to men which includes unbelievers as well as believers. God also says in Numbers 12:6, "Hear my words: If there is a prophet among you, I, the Lord, make myself known to him (or her) in a vision. I speak with him (or her) in a dream." Dreams can be given to heathen kings. Refer to Daniel 2:25-45.

Here are three examples of God communicating to people in a dream, vision and a trance:

1. **Matthew 1:20** – "Behold, an Angel of the Lord appeared to Joseph in a dream, saying,
   Joseph, son of David, do not fear to take Mary your wife, for that which is conceived in her is of the Holy Spirit; she will bear a Son and you shall call Him Jesus."
2. **Revelation 1:12 –15** – While the Apostle John was exiled on the isle of Patmos for sharing the gospel of Jesus Christ about 96 AD., Jesus appeared to John in an open vision for John was in the Spirit on the Lord's Day (of Judgment). John said, "Then I turned to see the voice that was speaking to me and on turning, I saw seven golden lampstands. In the midst of the lampstands one like the Son of Man clothed with a long robe and with a golden girdle or (sash) around His breast. His head and hair was white as wool, white as snow, His eyes were like flames of fire, His feet were like burnished bronze refined as in a furnace and His voice was like the sound of many waters."
3. **Acts 22:17** – When Paul, the apostle, went to Jerusalem to pray in the temple, he fell into a trance. Paul saw Jesus (in an open vision) speaking to him saying, "Make haste and get quickly out of Jerusalem, because they (the Jews or the people in general) will not accept your testimony about Me."

God still speaks to people in dreams and visions today. God speaks to me mostly in dreams and visions. God has given me the Seer gift of prophecy through dreams and visions, through the gift of discerning of spirits and through perception. I am able to perceive why people do what they do and say what they say as God reveals it to me. Sometimes, He does not reveal it to me.

God had given me a dream in the 1990's, in Oklahoma, where I lived for four years, while studying for the ministry at Rhema Bible Training Center. He revealed to me that revival was coming to America and that Bibles would be accepted in Public Schools in America. To my surprise, the President of the United States, Pres. Donald Trump, signed an executive order in 2017 to restore religious freedom in public places, such as in the public schools. He encouraged Bibles and prayer to be restored in Public Schools. In November, 2019, it was announced on CBN 700 Club by the CEO, Pat Robertson in Virginia Beach, VA, that Storybooks of the Bible curriculum were being read to and by children in the After-School Programs in the Public Schools in Richmond, VA. I also heard on the FOX News broadcast that Bibles and prayer were being restored in the Public Schools during free time in Florida.

God revealed to me in a dream an abundance of rain falling in dark city streets two times. Being a teacher of interpreting dreams and visions, God was telling me that the latter and the former rain of God's Holy Spirit or God's glory is going to pour out more on the earth. This means there will be a third awakening of the Church, who is sensitive to the move of the Holy Spirit that will invade the earth. To the remnant church, it will be a blessing; to those unbelievers who will not understand this spiritual event, it will be frightening. It will be a wonderful time for evangelism, to harvest souls, and for the Pastors of churches to disciple. I believe this event will occur before Jesus raptures the church, because there will be a time for restoration of all things stated in Acts 3:19–22.

Do not accept prophetic dreams from those people who have not accepted Jesus as their personal Savior, such as, Diviners, Mediums, Witches, New Ager, cult religions, etc., for they see visions that lie. They tell dreams that are false, and they give empty consolations. Zechariah 10:2. They have an Anti-christ spirit. Do not consult them for wisdom. It is not of God's wisdom.

- **SPONTANEOUS IDEAS OR THOUGHTS:** God speaks to you by revealing thoughts and ideas to you to solve a problem, to fulfill a call into the ministry, to give you ideas of songs to create, to instruct you on how to create an invention, or give you spontaneous thoughts about writing a book or playing an instrument. Whatever God gives you thoughts or ideas about, it is up to you to follow through by faith to pursue it with perseverance. He can give you thoughts and ideas that you have not been thinking of. Acting on these thoughts and ideas and expecting them to happen, activates your faith, called *the God-kind of faith*. The God-kind of faith is that measure of faith you received as a gift from God, when you received Salvation by Jesus Christ. The revelations God gives you through spontaneous ideas or thoughts, dreams and visions, a still small voice or an inward witness of anything, anyplace or anyone, are things hope for and the things that are not seen yet, but will soon manifest in a day, month, 6 months or up to 10 years. What God reveals to you in any way, know that He will bring it to pass. Hebrews 11:1 says, "Now faith the substance of **things** (anything God reveals to you) hoped for, the evidence of **things** not seen (has not manifested yet, but it will soon come to pass).

- **HEARING AN AUDIBLE VOICE OF GOD:** Very rare do you hear God speaking this way like a person in real life speaking to you. God only speaks to us this way when He sees we are about to encounter danger. Or you may be about to make the wrong decision unknowingly and you may hear God say a loud, "No!!!" You would think that someone behind you said "No." Obey that voice or suffer the consequences. However, God will speak to you mostly by way of the inward knowing guided by an inner peace. If you do not have peace about a decision or about a situation, obey that feeling. You will be glad you did obey. God will also speak mostly through dreams and visions.

- **GOD COMMUNICATES TO YOU OUTWARDLY:** God can communicate with us through the following ways:

- **CREATION:** In the beginning, God created the heavens and the earth. Genesis 1:1. After there was war in the third heaven between Lucifer (who became Satan) and his followers, one third of the angels (the fallen angels) were defeated by the archangels of God, and Satan and the fallen angels were thrown out of heaven to the earth. As a result, the heavens and earth became dark and void, Isaiah 14:12-17. God had to recreate the heavens and the earth within 6 days, Genesis 1:31-2:1. I and some theologians believe in the "Gap Theory" between Genesis 1:1 and Genesis 1: 2, because God began creation perfectly and with beauty. Something happened between Genesis 1:1 and Genesis 1:2 to disturb the heavens and the earth and to make them dark and void. After five days of recreation of the light, the firmament, the land, the sun, the moon, the stars, grass, trees, fruit trees, herbs, fish, and animals, God made man out of the dust of the ground on the sixth day. He said in Genesis 1:26, "Let us make man in our image, after our likeness and let him have dominion........" (dominion over what God created on earth).

God said, "Let US make man in OUR image, after OUR likeness...." This part of Genesis 1:26 involved two other persons in the creation and lastly in the creation of man who was called Adam. Those persons were THE LORD OR THE CHRIST OR THE WORD and the HOLY SPIRIT who lived before the world was, John 1:1-3, 14. Jesus Christ, His earthly name, is the Lord and the Word of God who spoke the Mind of God, His Father in Words and the Holy Spirit manifested the spoken words of creation. Isn't that awesome? God is still creating today through the Son, Jesus Christ, The Lord and by the Holy Spirit as He manifests what is spoken by Jesus Christ and the Father, God. The Godhead still is creating human babies in mothers' wombs, galaxies or milky ways consisting of billions of stars, individual stars, volcanoes, canyons, trees, flowers, mountains, He reveals inventions in people who are sensitive to God's Spirit. He gives creative ideas to people and those ideas are soon manifested through people with the help of the Holy Spirit. God's Word, through the Son and the Holy Spirit, set the recycling of the seasons and keeps the earth rotating on its axis by His creative law of gravity.

- **GOD'S WRITTEN WORD:** God's written word in the Holy Bible is called the logos that becomes alive or becomes a revelation knowledge once the reader applies the written

Word in His life by faith. Once the logos Word of God is applied by faith, one's heart or spirit is enlightened. The Word becomes a Rhema or enlightened Word in the spirit of man. The Word, read and spoken out loud, mixed with faith, becomes alive and the promise written in the Word or scripture is manifested, sometimes instantly or gradually.

The Holy Bible was written by the Holy Spirit, through sensitive prophets, as they were moved or inspired by God's Spirit. 2Timothy 3:16 (EBV) says, "All scripture is inspired by God and profitable for teaching, for reproof, for correction and for training in righteousness, that the man of God may be complete and equipped for every good work." 2Peter 1:20, 21(EBV) says, "First of all, you must understand this, that no prophecy of scripture is a matter of one's own interpretation; because, no prophecy came by impulse of man, but by men moved by the Holy Spirit spoken from God."

Through the written word, God can speak to you concerning how He can direct you by the examples of stories of characters. He can tell you how to conduct your life, give you guidance on how to solve everyday problems, describe who you are in Christ and what you have inherited in His Kingdom that is yours through Christ, as you mature by the Spirit of Christ. I apply Psalms 91 in my life and speak it out to my body. To this day, I have experienced and still am experiencing protection from the Father against extreme diseases, and if I catch a cold, he delivers me from it using herbs. No evil comes near the dwelling of my body nor my house, therefore, I don't need to have home protection alarm system, such as, ADT, etc. God sends angels to protect me wherever I go and to travel safely. Hallelujah!!! It is through His Word in Jeremiah 1:4-10 that God called me into the prophetic ministry and gave me the steps to take to study and develop the prophetic gift.

It was through the study of the characteristics of the end of the Church Age, that I learned what would be the signs of Jesus Christ's returning to rapture His faithful believers:

11

Matt. chapters 24 and 25, Luke chapter 21, 2Timothy 3:1-9, 1Thessalonians chapter 4:13 – 18, and the last whole book of Revelation. As a growing prophet, I need to know about the events that will occur in the last days of the end times. This study is called *Eschatology*. It pays to study the Word of God so you will know how to live in this fallen world, how to conduct yourself, and how to be protected. Be aware of events that happened in the past, so that you can learn from them and know the events that are to come while being prepared for the coming of Christ.

- **PROPHETIC PEOPLE AND MINISTERS:** God can speak through ordinary believers prophetically. He can operate any method of prophecy through adults and children who are sensitive to the unction of the Spirit of God. They do not have to be prophets, unless God has called them into the ministry of a Prophet.

God says in Joel 2:28,29 (EBV), "And it shall come to pass afterwards (in the last days), I will pour out my Spirit on all flesh; your sons and daughters shall dream dreams, your young men shall see visions. Even upon the menservants and the maidservants in those days (last days of the end times) I will pour out My Spirit." Paul says in 1Corinthians 14:5, "Now I want you all to speak in tongues but even more to prophesy. He who prophesies is greater than he who speaks in tongues unless someone interprets so that the church may be edified."

- **SPEAKS THROUGH CIRCUMSTANCES:** God speaks to us through a word of wisdom on how to solve a problem, or get out of a problem, because of a mistake we have made, or because of the mistake of someone else. God can correct us by His written word or by a conviction felt in our hearts or human spirit that will lead us to repent and ask for forgiveness. God will be faithful and just to forgive all of our sins or mistakes and at the same time, we are to forgive ourselves. God does not condemn you for making mistakes, but He will convict you to repent of the sin and move on with Him to enjoy life, as well as continue on to live in who you are in Christ. You are still God's special person who is growing into the image of Christ day by day. The Bible says in Revelation chapter 3:19, "Those whom I love, I reprove and chasten so be zealous and repent."

God develops and stirs up a character of love and care through circumstances, such as, stirring up the love He placed in you when you see a homeless person, child or even a stray or abandoned dog or cat in the streets. A believer should minister the gospel of Christ and give money for food to the homeless person or give him information concerning where the homeless person can receive shelter and food. If a dog or cat is abandoned, either you can call the ASPCA to pick up the animal or if you can, call the police at 911 to pick up the animal and find the owner of the animal. If the owner cannot be found, if you are led and you desire to keep the animal, that is up to you. My experience was seeing a helpless white dove, who injured his wing, and fell into the pit of my home near the basement windows. I immediately went to my basement and opened one of the windows to pick up the dove, but the dove would not allow me to touch him. I said to the dove, "Ok, you don't want my help?" I then shut the window. With my back turned to go back upstairs, I heard the tap on the basement window. It was the dove tapping his beak on the window. I opened the window saying, "Now you want my help?" The dove allowed me to pick him up and put him in an available cat carrying case I had stored in my basement. I took the dove to the ASPCA in Brooklyn, N.Y. The clerk accepted the dove and called her "Olive" and I left the dove there. How the clerk took care of the dove, I do not know, but I prayed that the dove would be taken care of. God stirred up love within me to help the dove he created. It was a lesson that this is how I am to deal with those who are helpless and homeless of which I do, as I am led of the Spirit of God. Jesus said in His Word in Matthew chapter 25:40, "Truly, I say to you, as you did it to one of the least of these, my brethren, you did it to Me."

God can use the life of an animal or birds to show how the mother and father bird take responsibility of caring for their young. They form a nest as their home and feed their young chicks. Through observing this, God teaches the importance of having a family, stressing the responsibilities of the father and mother in caring for their children. As you can see in the reports of the news media in these last days, families are declining in societies all over the world. Some children are without fathers and/or mothers, either because of death or divorce situations. In some societies, the traditional family with a mother and father having children has deteriorated because of adultery, homosexuality and transgenderism. This is the characteristic of what would happen in the last days of the end times, prophesied in the Word of God, the Bible.

Believers in Christ know the importance of having a family the right way, the traditional way, a more stable way if children are involved. They have the care and support of having a mother and father to care for them and love them. It is important for all believers in Christ to live by the dictates of the Holy Spirit within them and, according to the written word of God, to love one another, yes, even our enemies, those who are against the traditions of the faith of Jesus Christ. Paul says in Romans chapter 12:20, 21, "If your enemy is hungry, feed him or her. If your enemy is thirsty, give him drink, by so doing this, you would heap burning coals upon his head (or your enemy would feel ashamed for what he or she has done to you). Do not be overcome by evil, but overcome evil with good."

- **THROUGH SIGNS OF THE TIMES:** God is still in control of what He allowed and what He made happen in past history concerning the rise and fall of kingdoms and nations, what He is doing in this present age concerning the rise and fall of governments and judging of churches, and what He prophesied- the events that would happen in the future. It is important for all believers in Christ to be aware of what God has done in the past through His written word, what He is doing and allowing during this Church Age, what He will do and allow to happen in the future, in order for His prophecies to come to pass. What he says will happen in His

Word and what He reveals to you prophetically will come to pass. It pays for all believers to pay attention and not to be complacent about what is happening around them in their society and communities. We believers must be like the tribe of Issacchar, for they knew as prophetic seers, the signs of the times concerning what was happening and going to happen in their community and in the Davidic government, so that they would know and tell the other 12 tribes what to do and the importance of keeping in the faith using the wisdom and knowledge of God's commandments to stay safe physically, economically, and spiritually, preparing for the arrival of their Messiah.

What is happening today, in the societies and nations, especially in America, is that they have turned their backs on God, and therefore, societies are deteriorating socially, morally and physically. What is happening today can be compared to the evil days of Noah and the sexual immorality days of Sodom and Gohmorrah. Jesus Christ, when He walked the earth, prophesied and said in Mathew 24:37, "As were the days of Noah, so will be the coming of the Son of Man (who is Jesus Christ's coming). Luke 17:28, Jesus said, "Likewise, as it was in the days of Lot(who lived in the city of Sodom and Gohmorrah where sexual immorality flourished), they, the people, ate, drank, they bought, they sold, they planted, they built, but on that day Lot (and his wife and daughters) went out of Sodom and fire and Sulphur rained from heaven and destroyed them all (the people), so will it be when the Son of Man will be revealed (Jesus Christ will come)."

Paul said to Timothy in 2 Timothy 3:1, "In the last days, perilous times will come….." We are living in those times today. God wants all believers to be aware of the signs of the times that tell of Jesus Christ's coming to rapture the church out of the earth which is very close, even at the door. When you see signs increasing, such as the decline of moral values and sexually immorality in our societies, abortion, rebellion against all authority, many falling away from the faith of Jesus Christ, pestilences, earthquakes, tornadoes, hurricanes, the set up of a one world government, and dependency on government instead of on God through socialism and communistic governments, the rise of cults and occultism. When you see that Israel has become a nation and is flourishing, and that a multitude of Jews from the four corners of the earth are returning back to their homeland, Israel, and the gospel of Jesus Christ is being preached to the nations, Jesus Christ said in Matthew chapter 24:33 that when you see these signs happening, know that His coming is near, even at the door.

God wants all believers to be alert of the signs of the times of our day so we would know what to do to prepare for the coming of our Lord Jesus Christ. Before His coming, God is going to pour out the former and the latter rain of His Glory. This will be the last movement of the Glory of the Holy Spirit upon all flesh. All believers are asked to be prepared for this move of God by staying in the faith of Jesus Christ, abiding in Him, worshipping Him, staying faithful to doing the things of God as He leads you, like evangelism, prophesying to edify, exhort and comfort those who are in despair, and assembling yourselves with other believers. You would want to be counted worthy to be ready for the coming of Christ, who is coming like a thief in the night, to rapture or snatch those who remained faithful in Him out of the earth, to live with Him in heaven. The rapture will be a protection of true believers from the wrath of God called the Great Tribulation Period of seven years stated in 1Thessalonians 5:9, that will come upon the wicked unbelievers who have been rebellious against God and God's people. Let us Watch and Pray for we do not know the time or day when Jesus Christ will rapture the church body, but we can know by the signs of the times that His coming is very, very near. Let us be ready at all times.

- **GOD CAN SPEAK THROUGH THE USE OF TECHNOLOGY:** Did you know that God can also speak through technology as ministers preach on TV, Radio, iphones, cellphones, computers, and social medias, such as, on Zoom, Facebook, Instagram, Twitter, etc.?
  His messages of the gospel can be recorded on CD's, DVD's cassettes tapes, books etc. His gospel messages are going around the world through technology many ministers are using to carry out the gospel messages; some without leaving their homes or district location. Of course, there are missionaries

who are led by the Holy Spirit sharing the gospel to wherever they are called to go in the nations.

The prophet, Daniel 2600 years ago in Daniel 12:4 (EMB), an angel said to him, "But you Daniel, shut up the words and seal the book until the time of the end. For many shall run to and fro and knowledge shall increase." This prophecy is talking about our time today in which we are living in the tail end of the end times. Many people of God are travelling either as missionaries or as any of the fivefold ministries, either to attend Bible conference or taking the gospel to nations using jet planes, trains, boats, etc. Knowledge has increased through man in the invention of satellite technology through which ministers use to spread the word of God all over the world through T.V., computers, radios, etc.

- **GOD CAN SPEAK THROUGH THE SPIRITUAL GIFTS OF THE HOLY SPIRIT:** For the prophetic ministry, God will always speak through the Revelation and Utterance gifts or abilities or the manifestations of the Holy Spirit. Generally, there are 9 gifts or manifestations of the Holy Spirit that operate within any believer in Christ according to His will. Six of the 9 are as follows: **The Revelation Gifts or Gifts that Reveal Something:**

1. **Word of Wisdom** – The Word of Wisdom is the supernatural ability or manifestation of the Holy Spirit to reveal God's knowledge of His future plan and purpose for a person, place or thing. It also reveals God's Wisdom how to resolve a problem for the believer's protection or way of escape out of something or from something. The Word of Wisdom can be revealed within a believer's spirit as an intuition, in a dream or vision or still small voice or via the written Word of God. It can be confirmed through any minister of the fivefold ministry, or any Christian that is spiritually sensitive. Refer to Matthew 22:15-22 (Word of Wisdom came within Jesus Christ that kept Him from

being trapped by the Pharisees to have him arrested if he did not attribute taxes to Caesar, the emperor.); Ephesians 3:1-9 (Paul's future calling to reconcile the Gentiles to God was revealed.); Joseph, Jacob's son, had a Word of Wisdom in two dreams in Genesis 37:5-10 concerning his destiny to be the executor over all of Pharoah's land of Egypt and distribution of food during a seven year drought. It came to pass in Genesis 41:37-43.

2. **Word of Knowledge** – The Word of Knowledge is the supernatural ability or manifestation of the Holy Spirit to reveal of God's knowledge of facts or detail information of the past or present state or activities of a person, place or thing. This spiritual gift can be revealed by way of an intuition, or inward knowing, by a dream or vision, by a still small voice or by an empathetic feeling for the moment in a minister of healing of another person only for God to heal that person of the pain.
Refer to John 1:47-50 (Jesus had word of knowledge concerning the background of Nathaniel he saw under a tree before Jesus met him); Acts 9:10-12 (Ananias, a disciple of Christ, was given a Word of Knowledge the name of the street where to locate Paul in the city of Damascus, Syria and Word of Wisdom by which Ananias was given the future plan and purpose for Paul's life.)

3. **The Gift of Discerning of Spirits or The Distinguishing of Spirits** – The Gift of Discerning of Spirits is the supernatural ability or manifestation of the Holy Spirit to reveal to a believer different spirits in the spirit realm only. The believer is able to see, perceive and sense spiritually demonic activity, good or evil motives, discern the presence and voice of Jesus Christ or Satan, see angelic activity, hear angels singing, the trumpets playing and differentiate demonic intent from a human error or ignorance. This gift can be revealed also through dreams and visions. Refer to 1John 4:1,2 (always test the spirit to see if it is of God); Acts 16:16–18 (Paul discerns a spirit of

divination in a slave girl who was a fortune-teller and cast it out of her.)

The Utterance Gifts Or The Gifts That Say Something:

1. **The Gift of Prophecy-** The Gift of Prophecy is the ability to utter the inspired word of God. It is the bubbling forth-telling ability of the Holy Spirit within a believer to edify, comfort, and exhort a person or to a body of Christ in the attitude of love. Prophecy can come by way of dreams and visions, by way of a still small voice of the Holy Spirit, through trances, an inward knowing or intuition, a spontaneous thought or by the word of God. Any Christian can operate in the Gift of Prophecy as the Holy Spirit wills it. This does not mean that the believer is a prophet. However, prophets who are called into the governmental position in the body of Christ, can operate often in the Gift of Prophecy. Refer to 1Corinthians 14:1-5; 29 -33;39-40 (Any believer can operate in the Gift of Prophecy by the unction of the Holy Spirit.)

2. **The Gift of Diverse Tongues –** The Gift of Diverse Tongues is the supernatural ability or manifestation of the Holy Spirit to speak in various languages of different races or of an angelic language not learned nor studied, but only God or the person of that native language can understand when spoken to an individual or to a congregation, or to any group of people. In order for the people to be edified by what was spoken in diverse tongues, the Gift of Interpretation must follow it. There are two uses of the spiritual tongue:

    1. **The Devotional Tongue or The Speaking In Tongues-** This is acquired as a result of receiving the Baptism In The Holy Spirit. It is for the purpose of praying in the Spirit to God alone during your

devotional time with God and is for your building up your spirit man within and faith in God. 1 Cor.14:1-4; and Jude 20.

2. **The Gift of Diverse Tongue** – This kind of spiritual tongue operates through the believer as the Holy Spirit wills. It is announced like a trumpet with a loud voice to an individual, group of people or church congregation. This must be followed by the Gift of Interpretation so that everyone could understand what was spoken in the diverse tongue. Sometimes the interpretation can be given by the person who spoke the message in tongues or another believer who is sensitive to the Holy Spirit can give the interpretation of what was said in tongues, refer to 1Corinthians 14:5.

3. **The Gift of Interpretation** – The Gift of Interpretation is a supernatural ability or manifestation by the Holy Spirit that operates in conjunction with the Gift of Divers Tongue through the person who spoke in tongues or through another believer who is sensitive to the Holy Spirit to give the interpretation of the tongue that was spoken or through anyone who knows the language spoken in tongues can interpret the diverse tongue spoken.

   When the interpretation is given, it is giving a general meaning of what was spoken in tongues. It does not interpret word for word or translate what was said in tongues. Once the message in tongues is understood and it edifies, comforts and exhorts the congregation or recipient, then the message was a prophecy. Prophecy can be spoken through diverse tongues with the interpretation following,

The other three spiritual abilities of the Holy Spirit to make up the nine gifts of the Spirit are called The Power Gifts or the gifts that do something. They are **The Gift of Faith** which is God's power alone supernaturally given to a believer to expect all of the gifts of the Spirit to function within him or her without a doubt and with expectancy. It is a power gift that is different from human faith that uses your physical five senses expecting something by faith through experiences and the faith you received at salvation which is given as a measure of faith to use when expecting God to reveal and fulfil His spiritual promises inherited in the Salvation package. Gift of Faith is God's ability alone in operation according to His will through the believer having no doubt nor unbelief. The believer is given the ability to expect God to perform something instantaneously; **The Gifts of Healing** which is the supernatural ability of the Holy Spirit revealing through the minister of healing what to say to restore the recipient's body from any kind of sickness either through the laying on of hands or by speaking to the ailment. The results are usually instant. This gift is different from healing by faith by which the recipient recovers or the healing takes time to manifest, Mark 16: 18. It is not usually, instant. Sometimes but not all the time. And lastly, **The Gift of Working of Miracles** which is the supernatural ability of the Holy Spirit or God intervening into the course of nature for a moment or within a given time to cast out demons, replace a body part, open up the Red Sea, raise the dead, protect a person from danger or from a tragic accident without a scratch.

Definitely, the Gift of Faith is mostly operating in conjunction with the Gift of Working of Miracles for the believer to expect the impossible to happen in an instant. Matt. 9:23-25 (Jesus raised the dead in this scripture); Matt. 8:23-26 (Jesus controlling nature of a storm); Matt. 8:28-32 (Jesus casting out demons). Jesus said in John 14:12, that "any believer that believes in Him, the works that He did the believer can do too and even greater works."

However, generally, what was said before, the revelation gifts and the utterance gifts by the Holy Spirit can function along with the Gift of Prophecy. For example, the Word of Wisdom can be in conjunction with fore-telling of Prophecy in that it makes the prophecy to be more futuristic giving God's future plans and purpose for one's life that would edify or comfort or exhort or encourage a recipient with a sense of direction for his or her life. Through the Word of Knowledge, God may reveal facts about a recipient's background to help resolve a situation to promote emotional healing of the recipient. This can be comforting and edifying to the recipient giving him a sense of hope. Deliverance can come through the use of the Gift of Discerning of Spirits that can be edifying and encouraging to a recipient to be set free from certain demonic spirits of oppression or to know that guardian angels are supporting and protecting the recipient that could be comforting and edifying to know. And of course through the utterance gifts of Diverse Tongues followed by the Interpretation of tongues, recipients can be given prophecies that can edify, comfort and exhort or encourage.

CHAPTER 3

THE VARIOUS METHODS
OF PROPHECY

The purpose of chapter 3 is to help the believer in Christ to identify the methods God chooses to operate in him or her. As Paul, the apostle, said in 1 Corinthians 14:5, he wishes that all the saints prophesy. This means that whoever is born again in the spirit through the acceptance of Jesus Christ in one's life, and is filled with the Holy Spirit, or baptized in the Holy Spirit, God has given you the potential to prophesy at any spiritual level. However, even though you can prophesy, this does not mean you have become a Prophet, unless God by His Spirit has unction you or called you to be a Prophet as one of the fivefold ministries. To be a prophet, one must go through a process of being mentored, and it takes many growing years to develop into a mature prophet. It may take character development, emotional tests and instruction to become an efficient prophet. I will discuss more about what makes a prophet and the prophet's tasks in chapter 4.

The various methods God uses to communicate prophecy are as follows:

- **THE SPIRIT OF PROPHECY:** The Spirit of Prophecy is not a gift nor an office, but an anointing arising from the Christ within the believer that takes place on an occasion. The testimony of Jesus Christ expressed within the believer is the Spirit of Prophecy. When the Spirit of Prophecy is present and the anointing or presence of God is in the atmosphere, any saint can enter in and exercise faith to prophesy. Part of Romans chapter 12:6b says, "Let us prophesy according to the proportion of our faith." 1Corinthians 14:31 says, "That you may all prophesy one by one that all may learn and all may be comforted." Again, the Spirit of Prophecy usually occurs when the Lord's presence permeates in the atmosphere, especially during praise and worship or an anointed music is being played, making it easy for one to prophesy. It happens also when people come into the company of prophets or under a mantle of a prophet, Numbers 11:24-30; 1 Samuel 19:20-24.

- **THE GIFT OF PROPHECY:** The Gift of Prophecy is a gift and not an office. It is one of the nine manifestations of the Holy Spirit. He operates within any believer according to His will stated in 1 Corinthians 12:10 for the edification, exhortation, and comfort of God's people stated in 1 Corinthians 14: 3. The Gift of Prophecy is not based on Christian maturity. The Holy Spirit can operate His ability to prophesy through babes in Christ and through children, Acts 10:45, 46.

- **PROPHETIC PREACHING:** This type of preaching is done by the unction of the Holy Spirit concerning biblical truth. The speaker's words and illustrations are exactly what God wants to say. There is impact and accuracy in the delivered message. It is meant for the people in the congregation for that time. In such preaching, God wants to either prepare His people of what is to come, such as the rapture, or to encourage them that a breakthrough is coming, or to prepare for another wave of the Holy Spirit. At times, God may want to address the congregation about a concern of what is happening in the church that needs correction, Acts 2:14–21, Acts 3:19-22 & Acts 3:36-42.

- **PROPHETIC PRESBYTERY:** The Prophetic Presbytery is a gathering of proven ministers or prophets for the purpose of: 1. Giving prophetic revelation and confirmation of those who are called to leadership ministry in the church, Acts 13:1-3; 2. Ordains those who are called into the fivefold ministry, Titus 1:5; 3. Confirms and activates the membership ministries into the Body of Christ; 4. Progressing believers in Christian maturity by providing discipleship and ministerial training as well as providing experiences to develop their spiritual and ministerial gifts, as well as their natural talents, such as singing, dancing, playing an instrument, etc.

When I was studying for the prophetic ministry in my growing years into the prophetic, I studied under the tutelage of Rev. Pro. Christopher Cox whose prophetic teachers formed the presbytery. They anointed me to minister prophetically in music. Today, God has inspired me to establish open worship whenever I play the keyboard, as I am led of the Holy Spirit, at an assigned church, such as The House of Praise Church In Christ in Queens Village, N.Y. Sometimes, I may sing prophetically as a substitute musician.

- **THE OFFICE OF A PROPHET:** The Office of a Prophet can be either a female Christian minister called a prophetess, or a male minister, a prophet. It is a gift extension of Jesus Christ Himself as the Prophet within the minister. The prophet receives those attributes of Christ, giving her or him the ability to perceive what is in the heart of people, to proclaim the future, counsel the purposes of God, as well as know the secret things of God. Amos 3:7 says, "Surely the Lord God does nothing without revealing His secret to His servants, the prophets." More details about the Office of a Prophet will be discussed in Chapter 4.

- **THE PROPHETIC SEER OR THE SEER PROPHET:** All seers are prophets, but not all prophets are seers. To name a few, the following O.T. and N.T. prophets were seers: The prophet Samuel, Ezekiel, Daniel, Jeremiah, David's musician, Asaph, Psalms 83:3,4, David's prophet Gad (2 Samuel 24:11), Amos, Joel, Jacob's son, Joseph, Jesus Christ, the Apostle Peter, Apostle Paul and Apostle John- who wrote the book of Revelation.

To a prophetic seer, God shares His secrets through impressions, dreams, visions, through perception and the use of spiritual senses. Believers who often have dreams, visions, inward perceptions or who are sensitive to the spirit realm, can detect evil spirits or godly spirits, thus, they are called seers. God can share His secrets to believers in their dreams as they sleep; or by way of visions- either as open visions, with their eyes open, or inward visions, when they are half-sleep; or with their eyes closed while consciously awake, or reveal a vision in the back of their minds while their eyes are open and consciously awake. To some people, God communicates by way of the trance experience. This is when the person experiences the Holy Spirit surging His human spirit on a higher spiritual level, unaware of his surroundings, as the Holy Spirit reveals a vision to him or her. It is like the believer is experiencing an out of body experience while he or she is focusing on the vision from heaven. Sometimes, God speaks to the person in reference to the vision revealed. This happened to Peter in Acts 10:9-19.

As spiritual beings, seers would be able to see, taste, smell, touch and hear what is going on in the spiritual realm around us, just as we can in the natural realm. This gift can develop even more if we take the time to fellowship with the Holy Spirit through worship, by praying in the Spirit and studying His Word, so that more revelation knowledge can come to us spiritually. Seer prophets will be discussed in more detail when the Office of a Prophet is discussed in chapter 4.

CHAPTER 4

THE OFFICE OF A PROPHET

The Office of a Prophet is one of the ministerial gifts God has placed in the Body of Christ, the Church. It is one of the fivefold ministerial gifts that has a main task like the other ministerial gifts spoken of in Ephesians 4:11-14 that says (EBRSV), Jesus Christ has given, "Some Apostles, some Prophets, some Evangelists, some Pastors and Teachers to equip the saints for the work of the ministry, for building up the Body of Christ, until we all attain to the unity of the faith, and of the knowledge of the Son of God, to mature manhood (or womanhood), to the measure of the stature of the fullness of Christ so that we (as believers) will no longer be children tossed to and fro and carried about with every wind and doctrine by the cunning of men and by their craftiness in deceitful wiles."

Prophets are called into the prophetic ministry by God Himself or by Jesus Christ Himself to be a spokesman or spokeswoman for Christ. Some are called by birth like Jeremiah in Jeremiah chapter 1:4,5 and Samuel, when he was a boy in 1 Samuel chapter 3:3-19. As an adult, God can call believers into the Office of a Prophet by the Word of God, through a dream or vision, by a visitation of Jesus Christ Himself in a vision, or by a vision or actual visitation of an angelic messenger. Jesus Christ called me into the prophetic ministry as an adult, when I was inspired or impressed to refer to Jeremiah chapter 1:1-4. He called me into the teaching ministry by a dream, when God revealed to me fire proceeding out of my mouth before and when I was attending Rhema Bible Training Center in Oklahoma, where I studied for the ministry from 1990 to 1994. Ever since then, God has led me to attend several prophetic schools of which one of them was the Christian International School of Theology, under the tutelage of Prophet Bill Hamon and His assistant teachers, in Santa Rosa Beach, FL. Since then, I have come back to my home to live in Queens, New York.

There are 8 reasons a prophet must be isolated in the process of growing to be a prophet or a spokesman for God. Even though a believer is called into the Office of a Prophet, he or she does not become a prophet right away. There are emotional tests, a test of reliability, instruction and character development that one has to go through to be a mature prophet and a seer prophet. The 8 reasons are as follows:

1. To empty the love of the world out of the believer.
2. To strengthen the inner man through the study of the Word of God and pray more in the Spirit.
3. To be protected from the religious traditions and man made rules that are unscriptural.
4. To teach the prophets to discern or identify God's voice from other voices.
5. To learn how to interpret dreams and visions.
6. Once the prophet receives a revelation or message from God of direction, he or she must learn to be obedient and act or say the message according to God's guidance.
7. To establish rapport and fellowship with God as God shares His secrets.
8. To acknowledge and write down God's plans and purposes for the next assignment.

There are three types of prophets. They are as follows:

1. **A SEER** – A Seer is a prophet that functions according to what God reveals to him or her in the spirit realm. God may reveal things in the spirit through dreams and visions, through a perception and by way of the spiritual five senses. God reveals what is going on in the spirit realm to a Seer;

especially, seeing demonic activities in dark dreams. Seers can also see the Lord through a vision like the prophet Isaiah in Isaiah 6:1-8. Seers can see into the future like Joseph, Jacob's son, by interpreting the dream of the King of Egypt, Pharoah, the first, that saved Israel and the Egyptians from a seven-year famine. Refer to Genesis 41:25-44 for this story.

God may reveal things coming upon a nation like He revealed to Ezekiel in Ezekiel chapters 37-39 concerning the nation of Israel. In Ezekiel 37, Ezekiel had a vision of the valley of dry bones of the people of Israel, upon which God wanted Ezekiel to prophesy over the dry bones for God to breathe on the dry bones to come alive again. In Ezekiel chapters 38 to 39, God reveals to Ezekiel, in a vision, the Gog and Magog war between the nations of the North such as, Russia, Turkey, Iran and other Arab nations, that will attack the nation of Israel for her oil resources, in the future of the last days of the end times, during the seven-year period of the Great Tribulation. The gift of prophecy and the gift of discerning of spirits, operated by the Holy Spirit, is more prevalent to a seer.

Other seer prophets of the Old Testament: Samuel (1Sam 9:19; 1Chron. 9:22); Hanani (2Chron.16:7); Jeremiah (Jerm. 1:11-15); Ezekiel (Ezek chapters 1-3); Jehu (2Chron 20:2).

New Testament seer prophets were John, the Apostle who wrote the Book of Revelation Jesus Christ and Agabus (Acts 11:27-30). There are more, but these we'll focus on.

2. **A NABI** - There are two types of *Nabi* prophets:
   a) A prophet that God inspires words or bubbles up words from the spirit of man for the believer to speak out. He becomes God's mouthpiece. As the prophet is inspired to speak the very words God gives him or her, the opinions nor additional words, should be added to the message. If God speaks two words through the prophet, the prophet speaks just that, two words. In this case, the gift of prophecy and the gift of diverse tongues, with the gift of interpretation, can operate in this type of prophet.

b) Another type of *Nabi* prophet is one that hears the word of the Lord while he or she ministers to a congregation. God actually tells the prophet what to say. The expression used by Jeremiah in Jeremiah 1:4 says, "The word of the Lord came to

c) me." In other words, Jeremiah heard the Lord speak a word in his spiritual ear. Another expression is, "I heard the Lord say…." or "the word of the Lord came to me saying…" What he or she heard the Lord say cannot be mixed with his thoughts nor opinions.

The few Nabi prophets are: Jeremiah (Jerm.1: 4, 9,10), Jesus Christ, Agabus, Acts 11:27-30, Ezekiel 7:1, Haggai 1:3.

[1] **A PROPHETIC WATCHMAN CALLED A SHAMAR** – The Hebrew word *Shamar* is a watchman prophet to keep, guard, observe, and give heed. There are 3 types of watchmen in Hebrew. They are:

a) Natsar – to protect, observe, preserve, to see hidden things.
b) Shamar - to keep, protect, guard and preserve.
c) Tsaphah – to lean forward and peer into the distance, to keep watch, spy. This word is most often used.

The primary function of a watchman is to see, say and to pray. He or she sees and watches the plan of the enemy. In Isaiah 62:6, "On your walls, O Jerusalem, I, the Lord, have appointed watchmen, all day and all night they will never keep silent. You who remind (come into agreement with) the Lord, take no rest for yourselves."

Watching must be accompanied by praying and praying must be accompanied by watching. Ephesians 6:18 says, "praying

---

[1] Information taken from the Seer Anointing Workshop taught by Pastor Barbara Rispoli on October 6, 2019

always with all prayer and supplication in the Spirit, being watchful….."

Some of the Watchman Prophets were Nehemiah 4: 7-15; Hebrews 13:17. All leaders are leaders watchmen, also Ezekiel, Jesus Christ and John, the Apostle were watchmen in the New Testament. They saw warnings and restoration for individuals, churches, communities, cities, regions, states, and nations. They see, hear and experience what most would consider weird, things in the Spirit Glory realm as a watchmen functioning as intercessors, warriors, Priests, kings and prophets.

THE TASKS OF A PROPHET

A prophet is a spokesman for God. He has the very person of Jesus Christ living within as the Prophet. The prophet admonishes, warns, directs, encourages, intercedes, teaches and counsels. He brings the Word of God to the people of God and calls people to respond. The Prophet can undertake a huge variety of roles. They are as follows:

1. **Pray –** The important task of a prophet is prayer. Because he or she knows the mind of God, he or she is in position to pray effectively. He or she has a clear picture of what God is doing. The prophet watches for the revealed Word of God and prays it into being. The prophet must not rest until God has fulfilled His revealed Word, Isaiah 62:6. This can apply to any prophetic minister.
2. **Receiving the Word of God -** The key role of the prophet is to wait in the presence of God to receive the message of God. God is sovereign. We cannot tell Him when to speak, however, we must have our ears open, hearing with anticipation.
3. **Suffering -** A prophet is called to suffering. For example, Jeremiah spent many years in captivity before his people were in captivity. He was often rejected, and ostracized;

he was even accused of being a traitor. Suffering made the prophets extremely aware of their human frailty, Jeremiah 20:7-12. Those who cause the suffering of the prophet will be judged. Suffering softens the prophet's spirit so that he or she can give a harsh word of God in a spirit of love.

4. **Worship** – The prophetic ministry can play an important part in worship. Prophecy that speaks of the glory and wonder of God will inspire his people to worship. 1 Chronicles 25:1-5 speaks of many prophetic musicians who were set aside by David for the ministry of prophesying to the accompaniment of musical instruments as part of the temple worship. They were professional worshippers and prophets responsible for leading the worship in the house of God. Those set aside were the sons of Asaph, Heman and Jeduthun and their sons for the ministry of prophesying accompanied by harps, lyres and cymbals..

5. **Encouragement** - Encouragement of the brethren was another aspect of the prophetic ministry. Silas and Judas, for example, encouraged and edified the church of Antioch in Acts 15:32. Prophets encourage leaders of their nations to act boldly. The prophetic ministry is to alert the church to the nowness of the Holy Spirit. It awakens us to the will and purpose of God for us in the present, as to what He specifically wants to do in us and through us.

6. **Foretelling the Future** – Prediction or the revelation of the future is part of the prophetic ministry. Through his fellowship with the eternal God, the prophet has access to the future. He becomes the seer who has insight into God's purposes. Whatever he or she sees for the future is always related to the present. The prophet warns of future judgments to people so that unbelieving people will change their behavior now. The prophet can speak future blessings that will give hope for the present.

7. **Gives Direction and Guidance** - Prophets bring the Word of the Lord to the Christians. Some Christians can get so caught up in the events of the world that they do

not see what God is doing. It is true that in times of crisis, it is very hard to see God's hand at work. This is when the prophet's direction and vision are given so that God's people will know what is happening and what they should do. Personal prophecy can refer to this and must be treated with caution or with God's wisdom. The gift of prophecy, in general, is not a directive to tell a person what to do or how to decide. It may come that way, provided that it confirms with the recipient's decision. God wants to lead His people by His Spirit and teach them how to hear God for themselves. It is wrong to be totally dependent on others for guidance. Many Christians have been led astray because they failed to get their own Word from God.

8. **Interpret Dreams and Visions -** Another important aspect of the prophetic ministry is the ability to interpret dreams and visions. Prophets are sometimes skilled in interpreting dreams. In Deut. 13:1, God regards prophets and dreamers as one and the same. John Paul Jackson, a former teacher of prophecy and who is deceased, had good teaching on the interpretation of dreams and visions, whom I have studied under for about 5 years.

9. **Correction and Admonishing -** Prophets cooperate with God in breaking down all that is not built on the true foundation of the Christian faith. They do this by announcing God's judgment. At the same time, they watch over all that God is building to see that it is built according to God's Word. The prophet's job is lonely. He must attack the root of the evil which goes very deep and affects everything. The prophet criticizes the root cause of the evil exposed by the prophet.

10. **Exposing Bad Leadership –** Bad leadership has done terrible damage in the church. In some churches such bad leadership has scattered their congregation members. It may be one of the reasons some churches seem empty or have less people attending. It has imparted sin in the camp and perhaps evil spirits to hundreds and thousands of ordinary people in the congregation who trusted their

leader and were vulnerable because they submitted to the leadership. When the leadership in the church is bad, the job of the prophet is to expose it. Churches should be led by a team of pastors, prophets and evangelists working together in submission to each other for the edification of the church body. The pastor should not be idolized to deter the congregation's focus from the true worship of God or Jesus Christ. Prophets should expose this problem.

11. **Announcing Judgment** – God raises up prophets to speak to evil people and nations to give an approaching judgment. God's purposes in judgment are clearer if a prophet announces them in advance. The prophet's declaration and intercession gives God authority to deal with the evil. When a situation turns sour and God needs to take action, His prophet announces God's condemnation of the evil. This prophetic declaration would give God permission to send the judgment event against the evil. The Prophet and judgment go together. Without the prophets, God has no authority to bring either the judgment, the prevention or warnings of the judgment against the evil.

12. **Warning of Danger** – The prophet is a watchman who warns God's people of coming trouble. For example, when Paul, the Apostle, was going up to Jerusalem, the prophet, Agabus warned Paul that he will face danger there. Agabus revealed this to Paul through drama when he used a belt to wrap around both of Paul's wrists as stated in Acts 21:10, 11.

13. **Interprets The Signs Of The Times** – The Prophet Seer is one who has understanding of the times. This seer has the ability to perceive and discern the spiritual significance of a situation and can give the Lord's perspective on a given situation. The Seer Prophet is made able to read the spiritual climate. He is also made able to identify the prevalent motivational force. This Seer's role is to see through the masks and veils of pretention, to expose man's folly and evil and for the sake of seeing the

34

poor and the needy through. This type of prophet acts like a watchman over men's hearts, to discern motivation, to pray, and call forth correction. The Seer is set over men's hearts to call them to heavenly living. This type of prophet as a seer, has the basic nature and realization of his commission to observe and be watchful. Such Seer Prophets have dreams and visions that stand on the walls of a nation, city, or community to see what God is doing in the spirit. They see in the spirit what is coming through revelation knowledge given by the Holy Spirit.

14. **Prophets Must Test Prophecy** – Prophets make sure that when prophecies are spoken, they line up with the Word of God, they execute the character of God, and they confirm with God's Word, already spoken to the recipient or group of people or Pastor. If some of the prophecies do not confirm with the recipient, the recipient has the option of sitting on the prophecy, or taking it to God in prayer until it comes to pass (within at least 20 years or less) or ignore it if it does not come to pass.

15. **Challenging The Nation** – The primary role of a prophet is to speak to the people of God. With the permission of the Pastor, the prophet brings both direction and correction to his church. The prophet may be called to speak to a nation or to a leader of a nation. The O.T. prophets confronted kings and took important roles in national affairs as well as foreign affairs.

16. **Prophets Advise Kings and Political Rulers** – Some prophets are assigned by God to advise kings and rulers. When God wanted to guide a ruler, He would give that guidance through a prophet. Kind David had Nathan, the prophet as well as the seer, Gad to advise him.

17. **Initiating God's Action** – God does nothing without warning His people first through prophets. Part of the prophetic role is to release God's activity by providing these warnings.

18. **Prophets Explain What Must Be Done** – When a prophet receives a warning of a tumult event or the next

move of God coming as a third awakening, their task has just begun. They are to find out what God plans to achieve through the event and His strategy for the people who want to participate in His purpose during the event.

19. **Theology** – A prophet should be a theologian; he should know the Bible. Not only do prophets know the Word of God, but like Seers, they are men of revelation. All prophets Nabis and Seers are of enlightenment and intellectual maturity. All are involved in being theologians.

20. **Healing The Sick** – God uses some prophets to heal the sick. For example, the prophet Elisha was moved in the gift of healings in 2Kings 4:32-35 and in 2Kings 5:7-10.

21. **Appoint and Anoint Leaders** – In a godly nation, or in a church setting, prophets may have a role in the appointing of political leaders. Prophets may be a part of a presbyterial group to anoint other prophets and ministerial leaders for the ministry.

As you can see by the tasks of a prophet, that a prophet has a governmental role along side with the Pastor of a church if the Pastor allows it. However, a prophet always respects the leader of a church, as well as ask permission to give a prophetic word to Pastor's congregation. Whether a pastor accepts a prophet in his church or not, the prophet should not give up his or her calling as a Prophet even if it means to prophesy to ordinary people in the streets or to a Christian friend or family member. A Prophet always commune with God in prayer for your assignments.

OTHER VARIOUS PROPHET ASSIGNMENTS

1. **Governmental Prophets-**
   In The Old Testament:
   A) **Moses To Pharoah of Egypt** – "To let My people go" Exodus 9:1
   B) **Nathan, the prophet to King David of Israel** – "When your days are complete, your offspring of a son will build a house for My Name." 2 Samuel 7:12

C) **Elisha, a prophet to Jehosophat** – "The Lord will give you the Moabites into your hand...." 2Kings 3:18,19

D) **Gad, Seer Prophet to King David of Israel** – "Select for yourself what I may do to you." David took a census of how many he had in his army in order to win a battle instead of entrusting God for his victory winning battles. Therefore, God gave David through the Seer, Gad, 3 choices to judge the camp of Israel: 1. One to three years of famine; 2. Two to Three months of being swept away by the enemies; or 3. 3 days of pestilence throughout all the territories of Israel.

E) **Samuel, the prophet to King Saul, the first king of Israel** – Samuel encourages Saul that his donkies were found after three days of searching for them and reminded Saul his responsibilities over the desires of his Benjamite family matters of which Saul complained in 1 Samuel 9:19,20.

In The New Testament:

A) **John, the Baptist to King Herod of Judea and who renovated the second temple** – When John, the Baptist was put in prison by King Herod, John accused Herod of adultery for divorcing his first wife to marry his niece, Herodias in Matthew 14:1-12.

B) **Agabus, the prophet to Paul, the Apostle-** Agabus, who was from Judea, came to Paul and bound his own hands using Paul's belt and said, "In this manner, the Jews in Jerusalem shall bind the man who owns this belt and deliver him into the hands of the Gentiles," Acts 21:10,11.

C) **Jesus Christ executed the Government of the Kingdom of God** – Jesus preached the Kingdom of God with authority to all who heard Him. Even to the Pharisees and Sadducees who were defensive against His teachings.

2. **Selected Prophets over the Economy –**

    A) **Joseph, son of Jacob-** Joseph was given the Executive position by the Pharoah, Sesostris II, 1894-1878 BCE (information from Biblewise.com) over the possession of and selling of grain in Egypt to all those who needed because of the famine in the land; even to the family of Jacob that travelled to Egypt for food. Genesis 41:53-57.

    B) **Amos, the prophet-** Amos, one of the minor prophets in the Old Testament, dealt with the injustices concerning the economy in Amos 5:10-13.

    C) **Solomon, also a prophet of The Book of Proverbs** – Solomon knew how to get wealth in Proverbs 10:4,5.

CHAPTER 5

THE PITFALLS OF A PROPHET

[2]The **Pitfalls for the Prophetic Ministry:** A prophetic ministry must be ware and don't fall into the following traps:

1. Saints do not choose their membership ministry within the Body of Christ. It is God or Jesus Christ's sovereign choice to call you into the ministry of the fivefold ministry, 1 Corinthians 12:18 and Ephesians 4:11
2. Allow the Holy Spirit to illuminate your mind and soul to any character flaws, bad attitudes and root problems.
3. Prophets are sometimes rejected by church leaders, as well as persecuted and misunderstood, so your gift of prophecy may be ignored.
4. Some prophets who may not be emotionally mature can become disappointed, which in turn can soon lead to discouragement, resentment, self-pity, then to having a persecution complex and lastly, to anger. In this case, the immature prophet can get into spiritual error, especially if he or she thinks and says he is the only one left to preach a pure faith message. If such a prophet is not checked, he can take a truth and turn it into a cult and lead followers astray, (like what happened in the case of false prophet Jim Jones' ministry that cost the lives of his followers in a mass suicide in his jungle commune in Jonestown, Guyana in the 1970's).

---

[2] "Prophets Pitfalls and Principles" by Bill Hamon pgs 14 – mid 16.

[3] OTHER PROPHETIC PITFALLS:

1. **FRUSTRATION AND BITTERNESS:** All prophets experience rejection of their words in that their words are not always accepted and obeyed. This can frustrate a prophet and can lead to bitterness. Prophecy spoken out of frustration and bitterness can make the prophecy impure. Prophets must learn to deal with rejection without going into frustration and bitterness.

2. **ANGER:** Prophets can get angry with those who do not receive their words, especially if the prophecy given was not understood and was not true. People will not respond. Prophets must take heed how they present their prophetic message so that it is understood.

3. **PRIDE:** Prophets usually lead lives that are extremely righteous. They can easily take on the spirit of the Pharisees who felt good, because they could see the sins of other people and not their own. Pride is very destructive of the prophetic ministry. It pays for a prophet to prophesy with humility, wisdom and understanding when ministering to other people.

3. **PROPHETIC PUSHINESS:** Prophets must avoid the trap of pushing their name forward. Prophets must be servants of God's Word. Their only concern should be that God's Word is heard. If the Word is heard, it does not matter if the prophet is forgotten.

4. **REBELLION:** Pride often leads to rebellion. Rebellion is terribly crippling for a prophet. It is the moral equivalent of witchcraft, 1 Samuel 15:23. If you can't sit under authority today, you will react the same way to a future authority of a leader, so deal with rebellion immediately or you will miss out.

5. **CONTROL AND MANIPULATION:** The Jezebel spirit uses manipulation and control to achieve results. Prophets must avoid all temptation to help the fulfilment of their words by manipulating people. Steer clear of the 3 C's –

---

[3] "Prophetic Pitfalls" by Kingwatch.Co. N2 of Kingdom Watcher Ministries in New Zealand

Condemnation, Control and Criticism, when prophesying. These three words need to be rooted out of the prophetic words, in our thought life and in our actions. Don't give them a place by praying about them, thinking about them nor speaking about them. Stay linked to God's heart. Declare His heart. Be patient and proclaim His prophetic message. God will vindicate you in the end.

6. **MISUSE OF POWER:** Prophets can misuse their gift. Prophets must not use their gifting to protect their role or their reputation. Let God lead you to operate in your gift when it is necessary, especially when God assigns you to go somewhere to minister. Whomever you minister to, do it with humility and love, not to prove yourself a prophet nor promote yourself.

7. **JEALOUSY:** Prophets can often become jealous of other ministries that seem to receive much more honor and acceptance. Jealousy can prevent you from hearing clearly from God. Prophetic people need to have the fear of the Lord operating in their lives much more than others (by Cindy Jacobs in her book, "The Voice of God" pg. 68).

8. **SEXUAL IMMORALITY:** John Paul Jackson warns that prophets need to be very careful about sexual temptations. Sometimes a prophetic person will begin to discern and feel what someone is tormented with. If the prophetic individual is lax in their time spent with the Lord, it would be difficult to discern between their own feelings and those coming from other people. Take everything to God in prayer to give you the strength to resist the temptation of sexual immorality.

9. **RATIONALIZING MISTAKES:** Some prophets are so worried about their mistakes that they refuse to admit them. No one is right one hundred percent of the time. Rationalizing or failing to admit our mistakes usually ruins credibility. Don't be afraid to admit you were wrong if you prophesied wrongly. It shows you have integrity and honesty. Just repent and ask forgiveness to the recipient and to God. Don't condemn yourself. Proceed to carry on as a prophet of God. People trust people (like prophets or ministers) who say

they were wrong ("Surprise By The Voice Of God", pg. 268 by Jack Deere).

10. **CALLING OUT SINS PUBLICLY:** Prophets should not publicly accuse individuals of sin. The gospel provides guidelines for dealing with Christians who sin. They should first be spoken to in private and in love ("Growing in the Prophetic" pg. 62 by Mike Buckle).

11. **MONEY:** Money can be the cause of prophetic blindness. Prophets should be careful about giving favorable prophetic words to those who provide them with financial support. Generally, it is better if prophets can be financially independent of the church and the community by trusting God for their financial source. God will take care of His own prophets. People will give willingly to a prophet who prophesies God's heart in truth, no matter how much they are willing to give.

12. **PEOPLE PLEASING:** People pleasing is a killer for all ministers, especially for prophets. Prophetic people who tell what people want to hear will lose touch with God (Galatians 1:10-12; Ezekiel 13:2–8).

13. **CONFUSING WISDOM AND PROPHECY:** A prophet must be able to distinguish between what they receive from the Lord and what comes from their own wisdom. If they are unable to distinguish the two, they are on a slippery slope leading to disaster. Prophets should be very clear about the source of their words.

Some ministers can handle success without being lifted up in pride, and endure rejection and failure without growing overly discouraged. God grants that we as prophets can learn to be praised for powerful prophetic performances without becoming proud, criticized, disciplined, and without developing a persecution complex.

Prophets must develop Christ's character which is able to receive both positive and negative responses with consistent grace. The only way the Last-Day prophets are able to survive is to maintain a proper attitude and stay in communion with the Lord Jesus Christ, whether we are received or rejected by the people, or by the leadership of a church. [4]

TRAITS OF A TRUE PROPHET VS A FALSE PROPHET

1. A true Prophet has the following traits:
   A) He or she that prophesies by the Holy Spirit and in line with the Word of God, edifies, comforts and exhorts or encourages either the congregation or individuals. He or she does not condemn nor discourages using the prophecy; but is spoken in love. However, sometimes the prophecy can warn so the recipient can make the right decision on to the right spiritual path.
   B) Again, he or she prophesies with humility and in love, 1 Corinthians 13:1-3.
   C) A true prophet prophesies exactly what God reveals to him or her Nothing added. Jeremiah 1:9 and Ezekiel 21:1,2
   D) He or she lives a holy and righteous lifestyle with their prophetic gift.
   E) He or she does not charge for his prophecy to a recipient nor to a pastor. He or she allows the pastor congregation or person to give a free will offering for their prophetic ministry. A prophet does not merchandise his or her prophetic gift, Matthew 10:6-8.

TRAITS OF A FALSE PROPHET

The traits of a false prophet are as follows:
   A) He or she wearing sheep clothing but speak contrary of what is written in the Bible, Revelation 13:11 and Galatians 1:10.

---

[4] "Prophet's Pitfalls And Principles" pg 19 under subtitle, "Receive Everything With Grace" by D

B) He or she may say the right thing of God using flattery remarks to manipulate and control people for the prophet's gain and benefit, Romans 16:17,18

C) He or she uses their prophetic gift for monetary gain. For example, the false prophet Balaam who used his prophetic gift promoting lies for monetary gain, 2 Peter 2:1-15.

D) He or she chooses to live a secular lives and still serve God. The person prophesies good things to please the recipients while living a lifestyle of the world, Jude verses 4,5

CHAPTER 6

PROPHETIC ACTIVATION EXERCISES

The purpose of this chapter is to help activate the prophetic giftings within you. In the process of the activation, you will learn and experience the ways God speaks to you and reveals things of His knowledge to you. It is important that whatever God reveals to you, you are to write it down or journal it. So, for these exercises, it is best to have a pen and a note pad at hand. I will begin giving you some exercises so that you can practice hearing God's voice in various ways when He answers you. When He answers you from within, you will know that God is alive within you by way of the Holy Spirit who abides with you and in you forever. Remember, God can answer by way of the inward knowing or intuition, a spontaneous thought that comes to your mind that was not there before, via a still small voice or whisper, via an inward vision or an imagination, an outward vision called an open vision with your eyes open, or through an impression. God can answer you in any one of these ways as you do the exercises. They are as follows:

IN RELATION TO YOURSELF:

1.   In your quiet time or devotional time with the Lord after you have prayed in the Spirit either with your supernatural language or in your native language for about 15 minutes, ask the Holy Spirit to reveal to you what is God's purpose

for your life. Once God answers you, write it down so when God's answer comes to pass, you can reflect on the prophecy and see when you wrote it in your journal.

2. Next, ask the Holy Spirit what God thinks of you. Write it down.

3. Ask the Holy Spirit what God's thoughts are about you in relation to the following objects:
   a) A light bulb
   b) A flying eagle
   c.) A white pearl necklace
   d) A red rose
   e) A crown with diamonds

4. Ask the Holy Spirit what color God associate you with and why.

5. Ask the Holy Spirit how are you like a lion?

6. Ask the Holy Spirit how are you like a tree?

IN RELATION TO OTHERS:

1. Ask the Holy Spirit to reveal something about a person you meet in the street, at a conference, or about a friend. Ask the Holy Spirit how to deliver the message or how you should pray for that person.

2. Ask the Holy Spirit to reveal to you an encouraging message for someone in the street, at a conference, in a Bible Study group, or to a group at a meeting.

3. Ask the Holy Spirit how you should bless someone today.

4. Ask the Holy Spirit to place someone on your heart to pray for or call.

5. Ask the Holy Spirit what is on Jesus' heart to pray about.

IN RELATION TO THOUGHTS OF NATURE:

1. When you think of a Christmas tree, what is God saying to you about what the Christmas tree represents?

2. Imagine a river flowing in a forest, what is God saying to you about Himself in relation to the river flowing?

3. When you imagine flowers of various colors in a green field of grass, what is God saying to you about Himself in relation to the flowers in the field?

4. Imagine a waterfall, what is God saying to you about Himself in relation to the waterfall?

5. When you imagine a mother bird and father bird taking are of and feeding their baby birds, what is God saying to you about Himself towards you?

6. Imagine seeing a bird using twigs to build a nest; what is God saying to you? What does the nest represent to you?

IN RELATION TO OUTSIDE HOME SURROUNDINGS:

1. When you see a lively sparrow sitting on a branch, what is God saying to you about that sparrow?

2. What message is God giving you when you see an abundance of rain falling outside your house window? How does the Holy Spirit relate Himself to falling rain?

3. What message is God giving you when you see branches of green leaves on trees?

4. What spontaneous thoughts come to your mind about God when you see a squirrel gathering acorns or food into his mouth?

5. What message is God revealing to you as to who He is when you see flowers open and facing the sunlight?

6. What is God telling you He is like, when the sunlight shines on your house and everywhere around your house?

7. What message comes to your mind of what God is saying when you hear birds around your house singing or chirping?

8. What message of God comes to your mind when you feel the wind blowing on your face?

I hope those exercises helped to activate the prophetic revelations of God within you, and that you were able to identify the various ways God speaks to you. Keep a journal of what God said to you in answer to your questions. Journaling tells God you honor what he tells you and that you trust Him with what He tells you from within.

God can respond to you as a prophet or minister and to the recipient you minister to in 7 ways:[5]

1. **The Prophetic Declaration -** A Prophetic Declaration is when words are spoken by God creatively; a prophetic declaration can decree a thing and things will happen. It operates by the gift of Faith with authority. It's a speech that activates the Kingdom.

2. **Prophetic Exhortation -** Prophetic Exhortation is used to inspire people to step into their destiny. It encourages people to take action in achieving the call of God for their lives and for the lives of ministers and prophets. Refer to Acts 15:30,31. In this scripture, Judas, a new disciple, and Silas were prophets who were sent to Antioch to warn the Gentiles via the reading of a letter exhorting the people not to eat things sacrificed to idols, from blood, and eat nothing that was strangled. If they do this, all will be well with them. The Gentile Christians were glad to hear the exhorting message.

3. **Prophetic Prayer Through Intercession –** God can prophesy the answer or solve a problem through intercessory prayer, through you as a prophet on behalf of yourself or the recipient.

4. **Via A Prophetic Song –** Prophetic songs are spontaneously inspired. They reflect the mood of God through singing and through the playing of instruments. There are prophetic songs to the Lord and from the Lord. God can respond to the prophet and to the recipient through a song He places on the heart of the prophet to sing out or on the heart of the recipient to sing out. His songs can be sung to a congregation for the edification of the people in the congregation. Refer to 1Corinthians 14:15.

5. **Personal Prophecy –** Personal Prophecy is most common when a prophet or minister ministers a comforting word to

[5] From the study of the series on the book and workshop, "The Prophet" by Prophet, James Goll, CEO of God Encounter Ministries.

a recipient, or a word of wisdom of God, to give guidance either to the prophet within himself, or to a recipient through the prophet.

6. **Prophetic Dreams and Visions** – God can also respond to the prophet and to the recipient through dreams and visions.

7. **Prophetic Action or Drama** – God can respond a prophetic message through drama. He can warn or direct or guide a prophetic word through acting out His prophecy to a recipient through the prophet ministering to the recipient. Refer to Ezekiel 5:1-5 and Acts 21:10,11

CHAPTER 7

IDENTIFYING THE MAIN PROPHETIC METHODS OPERATING IN YOU

In conclusion, this chapter will focus on the main prophetic methods you may have operated in when you did the prophetic activation in chapter 6. This chapter will help clarify and identify the prophetic method the Holy Spirit can operate in you and when you practice the activation in chapter 6. Just remember, when you do practice the activations in chapter 6, always stir up the Holy Spirit within you by praying in the Spirit in your native tongue or spiritual tongues for about 10 minutes, so that your spirit is sensitive to the promptings or unction of the Holy Spirit when He speaks to you in your spirit.

- When you find yourself inspired to sing in the Spirit or speak by the Spirit exalting and praising the awesomeness of Jesus Christ, or singing or speaking the truth about Jesus or God and/or speak or sing any scripture in the Spirit in an atmosphere filled with God's presence through worship with instruments, then you would know the Holy Spirit is operating the *Spirit of Prophecy* within you. The Bible says for the testimony of Jesus Christ is the Spirit of Prophecy.
- When you find yourself inspired or feel in your spirit an unction or prompting to say an encouraging, exhorting, edifying and comforting word in love to someone or a group

who may be depressed or discouraged, or one who may have low self-esteem, as well as one who may be going in the wrong direction in his or her life, then know the Holy Spirit is operating within you, as a believer, the *Gift of Prophecy,* when necessary, according to His will and in agreement with the will of God the Father and the Son, Jesus Christ.

- If you are a Pastor or Minister of a congregation or Bible group and you are inspired to correct, warn or prepare a sermon for your congregation or group expressing God's heart to prepare for a breakthrough, to solve and correct congregational issues, or to speak on spiritual events, such as, the rapture, or the outpouring of His glory and how your people must get their lives prepared spiritually for these events, then you will know, as a Pastor or a minister, that you are operating in *Prophetic Preaching,* because you are preaching what is on God's heart to your congregation or group.

- When you find yourself inspired to pray out a burden God placed on your heart for a friend, for a church leader, a leader of a nation, the people to receive salvation, a family member, and even for yourself. You pray frequently, praying out matters that are on your heart, know that the Holy Spirit is praying through you what is on God's heart for those people he places on your heart. This is referred to as a *Prophetic Intercessory Prayer.*

- When you find yourself inspired to sing, dance or dramatize a message from God to edify the body of Christ, then you are expressing God's song, dance and acting called *Prophecy Through Music and Drama.*

- Lastly, there are 21 reasons that you are growing into the *Office of a Prophet* when you find yourself doing the following:

1. You hate sin, but not people as individuals.
2. You have an urgency to warn God's people.
3. You are conscious of God's holiness. You take God seriously and must obey Him when he speaks to you.
4. You are against corruption of religion that makes God's word and Holy Spirit non- effectual.

5. You are against the traditions of men, again that makes the move of God non- effectual. As a result, church becomes dead in spirit.

6. Not a follower of the crowd, but a follower of Jesus Christ.

7. You are walking in who God called you to be, a prophet or prophetess.

8. You love to proclaim God's Word.

9. You are a creative thinker.

10. You love to be a leader of what God calls you to do.

11. You love to worship God, and you are a good discerner of true worship and the worship is anointed.

12. You love to speak the truth of God's Word.

13. With humility, you are conscious to live holy.

14. You put Jesus Christ first when making decisions.

15. It disturbs you when you see someone being taken advantage of.

16. You are usually misunderstood as being judgmental when in love you correct someone in righteousness.

17. Sometimes people will disrespect you when trying to relay the truth of the Word of God or sharing an exhorting prophecy. Do not be offended; bless the individual. Don't retaliate. Your character is being tested.

18. You love to write everything down that the Lord reveals to you as a spontaneous thought, dream, vision, an impression or a still small voice.

19. When God gives you a regional assignment and gives you words of wisdom on how to carry out that plan.

20. Prophets will suffer some rejection when carrying out God's message spoken to an individual, church leader, a group of people or a leader of a nation. Remember, don't get upset. Don't allow the rejection to anger you nor make you bitter. God eventually will vindicate you in time.

21. When you feel the urge to prophecy to someone, ask God how to approach the recipient to relay the prophecy; should you pray on it first. Follow the promptings of the Holy Spirit within you. You know you are growing

to be a prophet if you have no fear of making mistakes delivering a message you thought the Lord said. Through your mistakes, you are determined to hear God correctly and therefore able to deliver with confidence the correct message. Repent of your mistakes and carry on as a prophet or prophetess with confidence and in faith, knowing that Jesus Christ, the true Prophet is speaking through you and revealing things to you even if you are called to be a seer prophet. You will know that you are in the Office of a Prophet when God has positioned you to govern alongside a church leader, because you will have the respect and agreement of the leader. The prophet is to support the leader's vision for his or her church, as well as help edify, exhort and comfort his congregation with a prophetic word. Sometimes, God can call a prophet to be a prophet to a leader of a nation, or call that person to be a watchman over a nation to do intercessory prayer of protection, or to have victory over an enemy, etc.

In conclusion, it is hoped that after you have read this Simple Prophetic Handbook, you will have an idea of how God prophesies through you and that God has called you into the prophetic ministry. Even if He did not call you into the prophetic ministry, He perhaps inspired you to know something about the prophetic ministry. Again, the purpose of this handbook is for you to identify how God can use you to prophesy His message through you to edify, exhort and comfort a believer or unbeliever.

If you are a believer filled with the Holy Spirit, whether you know it or not you are a candidate through which God by the Holy Spirit, can prophesy through you using anyone or all of the prophetic methods spoken of in the Simple Prophetic Handbook. May you be blessed reading and doing the prophetic activation in this handbook.

RESOURCE REFERENCES

- PROPHETS PITFALLS & PRINCIPLES (God's Prophetic People Today) BY DR. BILL HAMON
  Published by Destiny Image, 1991 ISBN: 09399868059-#3
- THE PROPHET (Creating & Sustaining A Life-Giving Prophetic Culture) BY SEER PROPHET JAMES W. GOLL
  Published by Destiny Image, 2019 ISBN – 13: 978-0-1684-5044-6
- COURSE 101 ON "THE ART OF HEARING GOD" BY THE LATE, PROPHET JOHN PAUL JACKSON, CEO of The Streams International Ministries, formerly in New Hampshire, but moved to Texas.
- A TWELVE WEEK COURSE BASED ON THE BOOK, "THE PROPHET" BY SEER PROPHET JAMES W. GOLL
  Pastor of the God Encounter Ministries, in Tennessee.
- A SEMINAR OF THE TEACHING ON "A SEER ANOINTING" BY PASTOR BARBARA RISPOLI of The Healing Waters Church in Selden, N.Y.
- WEBSITE: Kingdomwatcher.co.nz/propheticministry/role.hp of The Kingdom Watcher Ministries BY RON MCKENZIE, EXEC. DIR.
- HOLY BIBLE (The Revised Standard Version), 1980 from the American Bible Society

MENTORS

Some of the prominent teachers Rev. Washington has been mentored by and who have been responsible for her development into the prophetic ministry are the following:

- Prophet and Seer John Paul Jackson (deceased on February 18, 2015), CEO of the Streams International Ministries, formerly stationed in New Hampshire from about 2005 – 2010, Streams International Ministry moved to Texas.
- Dr. Bill Hamon, CEO of The Christian International School of Theology in Santa Rosa Beach, FL. Major: The Prophetic Ministry from 2004 to 2009 to acquire a M.S. Deg. in Ministry as a correspondent student with few class attendances in Santa Rosa Beach, FL.
- Apostle and Prophetess Pauline Walley-Daniels, CEO of The Prophetic Deliverance Theological Training Institute in Bronx, New York. Rev. Washington received mentorship by Apostle Walley-Daniels at the Christ For The World Bible College in St. Albans, New York from about 2015 - 2019.
- Prophetess Teresa McCall-Gripper, CEO of The Naioth Prophetical Arts Institute, a School For The Prophets in Brooklyn N.Y. Mentored from 2017 – 2018
- Seer prophetess and Pastor Barbara Rispoli of The Healing Waters Church and CEO of the Healing Rooms Ministry in Selden, New York; Mentored in the seminar, "A Seer Anointing" in October, 2019.

MINISTRY RESOURCES WRITTEN BY
REV. SANDRA WASHINGTON

"Eschatology: The Signs of The Times Of Jesus Christ's Soon Return" was originally a title of a thesis that Rev. Washington was inspired to publish into a book format. She was inspired to alert the readers that Jesus' coming is closer than they think and that it is important for them to be aware of the signs of the times that tell of Jesus Christ's close return especially for those who receive His salvation.

This book will include the events that will occur during the Rapture, the Great Tribulation, The Millennial Age and the Perfect Age, define the meaning of each Age and discuss the signs setting the stage for each Age to come.

This book will also prove the validity of the Bible that contains prophecies that were spoken and written by the prophets in the Old and New Testaments. Some of the prophecies proclaimed of what will happen in the end-times by the prophets of old such as, Daniel, Ezekiel, Joel, Zechariah, Jesus Christ, John, the Apostle, Paul, etc., have already come to pass during the Church Age and during the history of Gentile nations until this day.

Rev. Sandra Y. Washington has been divinely inspired not only as a singer, author and teacher of the gospel, but as a developing prophetic seer in the area of dreams and visions with the developing ability to interpret them. It is her desire to write this handbook on understanding your dreams and visions for those who desire to understand the meaning of God's messages in their dreams as they learn the symbolic meanings of images in the dreams and visions and learn to rely on the Holy Spirit for the revelatory meaning of the dream and vision.

ABOUT THE AUTHOR

Rev. Dr. Sandra Y. Washington, a retired Classroom and Music Teacher of the New York City Board of Education for 21 years, has been called into the ministry by God in which she was to be trained as a minister of the Gospel at Rhema Bible Training Center under teachings of Dr. Kenneth Hagin Sr. and his staff near Tulsa, Oklahoma from 1990 – 1994. It was there in one of her evangelistic classes that God called Rev. Washington into the prophetic ministry, when she was inspired to turn to Jeremiah chapter 1, and when she had a dream of fire coming out of her mouth. She remained in Oklahoma for four years to do her internship under Pastor Clifton McDowell in Henrietta, OK., and Pastor Jimmy Cortez in Okmulgee, OK. It was under Pastor Jimmy Cortez's ministry that a visiting prophet named Prophet Alvin, prophesied to Rev. Washington that she would be a prophetess sent to churches that needed to be enlivened spiritually by the Holy Spirit.

In 1994, Rev. Washington sought employment as a Music teacher in private schools, such as Montessori School in St. Albans, N.Y. for two years, and Evangel Christian School in Long Island City, N.Y. for seven years. She retired in the year of 2004 to pursue her further training in the prophetic ministry and was inspired to start her own ministry called, The Great Commission of Jesus Christ Evangelistic Teaching and Music Ministry, Inc., which was later in the year of 2014 was changed to the Great Commission Multi-Service Community Center, Inc. It still remains as an outreach teaching ministry to edify the body of Christ, as well as those who wish to be part of the body of Christ in the areas of developing people who may have a prophetic calling, who may desire remedial reading and it prepares them for the coming of Jesus Christ through the teaching of the Signs of the

Times called Eschatology and Book of Revelation. She received her M.S. Degree in Ministry (majored in Prophetic Ministry) from Christian International School of Theology, Dr. Bill Hamon, CEO. in Santa Rosa Beach, FL and Doctorate of Divinity from The Canadian International Chaplaincy Academy, Dr. P. Phinn, CEO in Queens, N.Y. in 2018.

Rev. Washington was called into the prophetic ministry through the word of God stated in Jeremiah chapter 1: 4–10 and through a dream of fire coming from her mouth. In verse 10, God stated her mission eventually to happen. Like Jeremiah, God spoke to Rev. Washington mostly through dreams and visions as well as through perception. It is because of this, Rev. Washington sought training in the areas of interpreting dreams and visions and studies in the development of a Seer prophetic ministry. It is in her heart to share her training experiences in the prophetic with others who are interested in developing their prophetic giftings and interpreting dreams and visions. This is why she was inspired to write her book on *"The Simple Prophetic Handbook"* with the hope that Christians who have a prophetic calling can identify the various ways God prophesies through them. She also wrote a book called, *"Handbook on Dreams and Visions and How to Interpret Them"*.

www.ingramcontent.com/pod-product-compliance
Lightning Source LLC
Chambersburg PA
CBHW051240120626
46547CB00014B/1727